# Preventing and Treating Addiction

# YOU ARE NOT ALONE

OPIOIDS AND OPIATES:
THE SILENT EPIDEMIC

**Chronic Pain and Prescription Painkillers**
**The Dangers of Drug Abuse**
**The Heroin Crisis**
**Preventing and Treating Addiction**
**Who Is Using Opioids and Opiates?**

OPIOIDS AND OPIATES:
THE SILENT EPIDEMIC

# Preventing and Treating Addiction

XINA M. UHL

MASON CREST
PHILADELPHIA

**Mason Crest**
450 Parkway Drive, Suite D
Broomall, PA 19008
www.masoncrest.com

Printed and bound in the United States of America.

CPSIA Compliance Information: Batch #OPO2017.
For further information, contact Mason Crest at 1-866-MCP-Book.

First printing
1 3 5 7 9 8 6 4 2

Library of Congress Cataloging-in-Publication Data

on file at the Library of Congress
ISBN: 978-1-4222-3826-4 (hc)
ISBN: 978-1-4222-7966-3 (ebook)

OPIOIDS AND OPIATES: THE SILENT EPIDEMIC series ISBN: 978-1-4222-3822-6

## QR CODES AND LINKS TO THIRD-PARTY CONTENT

# Table of Contents

**KEY ICONS TO LOOK FOR:**

**Words to understand:** These words with their easy-to-understand definitions will increase the reader's understanding of the text while building vocabulary skills.

**Sidebars:** This boxed material within the main text allows readers to build knowledge, gain insights, explore possibilities, and broaden their perspectives by weaving together additional information to provide realistic and holistic perspectives.

**Educational Videos:** Readers can view videos by scanning our QR codes, providing them with additional educational content to supplement the text. Examples include news coverage, moments in history, speeches, iconic sports moments and much more!

**Text-dependent questions:** These questions send the reader back to the text for more careful attention to the evidence presented there.

**Research projects:** Readers are pointed toward areas of further inquiry connected to each chapter. Suggestions are provided for projects that encourage deeper research and analysis.

**Series glossary of key terms:** This back-of-the book glossary contains terminology used throughout this series. Words found here increase the reader's ability to read and comprehend higher-level books and articles in this field.

 **Words to Understand in This Chapter**

opioid—a natural or synthetic drug used for the relief of pain.

overdose—to take a lethal or toxic amount of a drug.

sobriety—the state of being free from drugs or alcohol.

*A 2017 study performed by researchers from Indiana University and the University of Virginia found that there is a direct relationship between the rising unemployment in an area and an increase in opioid addiction.*

1

# The Scope of the Problem

Nineteen year old Sean O'Conner became a heroin addict in high school. He was living with his aunt, uncle, and cousins--and stealing from them and their neighbors, too. He needed the money for his next fix. One night, he went to a friend's birthday party. He was anxious to get his next fix. As he waited he got drunk. When he shot up at last, he began to have seizures. The man who sold him his fix propped him up against a tree and went back inside his house, leaving O'Conner where he was. Luckily, a neighbor saw him outside and called the police. He woke up in an ambulance after medical personnel administered a shot of the drug naloxone to reverse the effects of a heroin *overdose*. They told him that he had nearly choked on his tongue because of the seizures he had been having.

O'Conner entered rehab. His mother told him, "Go and get better or you're done, no more family."

At first O'Conner was resentful and uncooperative, but then he realized the benefits of getting clean. Things would improve with his family, and he could get his high school diploma. He knew it would be a long road to *sobriety*, but he decided to go for it.

 ## Drugs at the Doctor's Office

Being a doctor is a hard job. Their schooling is long and expensive. Their internships and residencies often require long hours and tough decisions. Not only is it stressful to deal with patients' life and death diseases and injuries, but it's also tough to deal with their insurance companies. Doctors commit suicide at twice the rate of the general population. But that's not the only problem they have. Drug abuse is also rampant. Up to 10 percent of the general population is addicted to drugs and alcohol. This number climbs to 15 percent for doctors. This is due, in part, to physicians' easy access to prescription medicine. A 2013 study published in the *Journal of Addiction Medicine* reported that 69 percent of doctors had abused prescription medications. The reason for this abuse was to relieve stress and either physical or emotional pain.

When doctors descend into addiction they often head to rehab. There, for once, the percentages work for them. Studies report that they succeed at rehab programs between 70 and 80 percent, a rate that is quite high when compared with other that of others who attend rehab programs.

O'Conner is not alone in surviving an overdose. Many aren't so lucky, though.

## Hard Numbers

The Centers for Disease Control (CDC) has issued an alert about the epidemic of drug overdose deaths in the United States. More than six out of ten overdose deaths involve an *opioid*. Opioid overdoses have quadrupled since 1999. From 2000 to 2015 that figure equaled more than 500,000 deaths. That works out to a figure of 91 Americans dying each day from opioid overdoses. More than a thousand people a day are treated in emergency rooms because of misuse of prescription opioids.

In 2014 alone, drug overdoses claimed 47,055 lives. This is more than deaths caused by motor vehicle accidents (35,398) and firearms (33,599). Experts from Columbia University predict that the overdose deaths will continue to rise at least through 2017.

Clearly, something terrible is happening in the homes, schools, and workplaces of America. The opioid overdose epidemic has been fueled by an increase in the sales of prescription opioids for pain. They accounted for more than 183,000 deaths between 1999-2015. The prescription opioids most commonly abused are methadone, oxycodone (such as brand name OxyContin), and hydrocodone (such as brand name Vicodin). States with double-digit percentage increases in prescription opioid overdoses from 2014 to 2015 are: Massachusetts, New York, North Carolina, Ohio, and Tennessee. No state has escaped the scourge of opioid overdose deaths, though.

# Did You Know?

Among patients not suffering from cancer, 1 in 4 people who receive prescription opioids struggle with addiction.

## A Lethal Path

Many, if not most, opioid addicts start their road to addiction in the doctor's office, and the path they take is a familiar one. After a period of regular usage, it takes more opioids to achieve the same high as previously. A person's tolerance for the drug has increased. They must take more of the drug more frequently than before or suffer difficult withdrawal physical and emotional symptoms. These include headaches, trembling, chills, bone and muscle pain, insomnia, diarrhea, vomiting, nightmares, hallucinations, and depression. All of this is accompanied by an intense craving for the drug. Opioid use is about more than just experiencing the initial euphoria after administration. Now it is about avoiding withdrawal, too.

 ## Educational Video

Scan here to see a beauty-pageant winner talk about growing up in a family of addicts.

Addiction leads users to try to obtain more prescription pills from their doctor's office, or from multiple doctor's offices at once. Addicts frequently transition to buying opioids like heroin off the street. The cost becomes too high to sustain. Addicts begin to steal from family, friends, or neighbors. They may turn to prostitution or trade sex for drugs. Many are arrested, and ordered into drug treatment programs, or rehab. Often, individuals relapse, or begin to use opioids again. Rehab can be a revolving door. The most sobering statistic on addiction is that 90 percent of them start in a person's teen years.

Yet despite these grim numbers, there is hope to prevent further addictions and successfully treat already addicted individuals. Even the most desperate abusers have found help.

 **Text-Dependent Questions**

1. What has happened to the opioid overdose rate since 1999?
2. How do most opioid addicts begin their addiction?
3. What withdrawal symptoms do opioid addicts experience when they stop using drugs?

 **Research Project**

Visit the National Institute on Drug Abuse's Emerging Trends and Alerts webpage at https://www.drugabuse.gov/drugs-abuse/emerging-trends-alerts. Scroll down to the alerts, located in boxes with an exclamation point icon in the corner. Choose one of the alerts and write a one-page essay summarizing the issue.

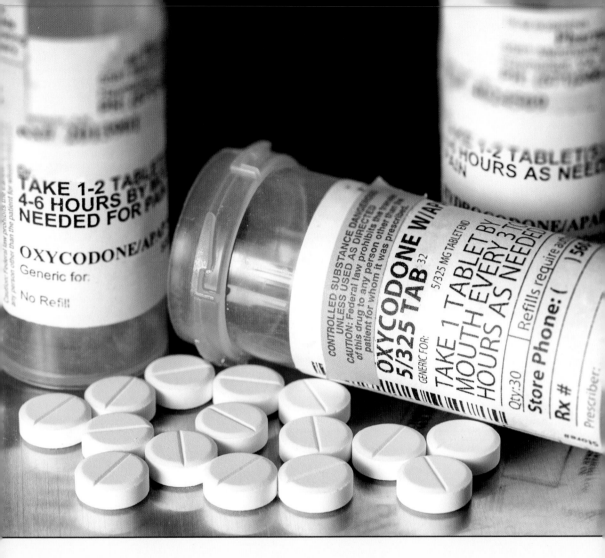

 **Words to Understand in This Chapter**

euphoria—to take a lethal or toxic amount of a drug.

narcotic—a natural or synthetic drug used for the relief of pain.

pharmaceutical—drugs taken as medicine.

stupor—a condition in which a person has dulled senses, difficulty moving, and generally is nearly unconscious.

2

# What's What With Opioids

The original opioid is the opium poppy, which contains a *narcotic* drug known as opium. Opium is the basis for some of medicine's most powerful painkillers. By itself, opium was used to relieve pain for thousands of years. Beginning in the 19th century, morphine was derived from opium. Other derivatives followed, like codeine. Semisynthetic opioids are created in labs from natural opioids. Examples are hydromorphone, hydrocodone, oxycodone (brand name OxyContin) and heroin. Fully synthetic opioids are completely man-made and include fentanyl, pethidine, levorphanol, methadone, tramadol, and dextropropoxyphene.

Opioid drugs work by binding themselves to opioid receptors in the brain, spinal cord, and other areas. Chemically, they resemble endorphins, or opioids that our bodies make naturally in order to relieve pain. Opioid drugs are able to reduce feelings of pain by reducing the sending of the brain's pain messages.

## Effects of Opioids

How quickly opioids affect a person has to do with how they consume it. Taking opioids in pill or tablet form causes them to travel through the digestive system. The drug is absorbed slowly because of this. Smoking causes quicker absorption of the

*An Afghan farmer holds the seed pod of an opium poppy. Juice from the seed pod can be refined into pain-killing opiates like morphine and codeine. A separate class of drugs, called opioids, are synthetic compounds that mimic the effects of opiates. These drugs include substances that are currently illegal in the United States because they have no medicinal value, such as heroin, as well as drugs that are prescribed as painkillers such as hydrocodone and oxycodone.*

**Spotlight on Fentanyl**

In the 1970s and 80s, synthetic opioids flooded the drug market. The most popular of these was fentanyl and similar drugs such as alpha-methyl-fentanyl (AMF) and 3-methyl-fentanyl (3MF). Particularly dangerous is 3MF which is said to be 1,000—3,000 more potent than heroin. Fentanyl itself is 50 times stronger than heroin and 100 times stronger than morphine.

The two types of fentanyl are *pharmaceutical* fentanyl that is legally manufactured. It is prescribed to manage acute pain and long-term pain such as that associated with fatal cancers. Non-pharmaceutical fentanyl is manufactured illicitly. It is often mixed with heroin, cocaine, or both in order to increase the drug's effect.

Synthetic opioids such as tramadol and fentanyl have become increasingly popular—and increasingly lethal. Deaths due to them increased by 72.2 percent during 2014-2015. These death rates occurred across age groups, races, education levels, genders, and regions. It is found in all states, but some states had particularly high usage during this time period. These include Connecticut, Illinois, Maine, Massachusetts, New Hampshire, New York, Ohio, Tennessee, and West Virginia.

drug because it is inhaled into the lungs, and then travels to the brain and spine. The quickest absorption of all is injection. It is immediately transmitted into the blood supply where it can almost instantly affect the brain and other body areas.

When opioids are smoked or injected the strongest effects take place in the first few minutes. A sensation called a rush

## Did You Know?

In 1914, the Harrison Narcotics Act was passed by Congress. It outlawed the sale of narcotics without a prescription. Prior to this, opiates appeared in many medicines—even those consumed by infants!

lasts for two to five minutes. How intense this rush is depends on the strength of the substance and how much is taken. Along with the rush comes a warm flush of the skin, dry mouth, and a heavy feeling in the limbs. If the dose is very high nausea and severe itching can result. After the rush comes a feeling of *euphoria*, a profound sense of well-being as though all a person's needs have been met. Dizziness, a dazed feeling, and *stupor* then results.

## Health Effects

We've looked at the drug's pleasurable effects, but what of other health effects? Heroin is one of the most potent opioids.

## Educational Video

Scan here to see a video on the factors that make addiction a disease:

*According to the Drug Enforcement Agency (DEA), abuse of prescription opioid pain relievers can lead to heroin use. Heroin is cheaper and easier to obtain and produces a similar high. Unfortunately, there has been a 286 percent increase in heroin-related deaths over the past fifteen years.*

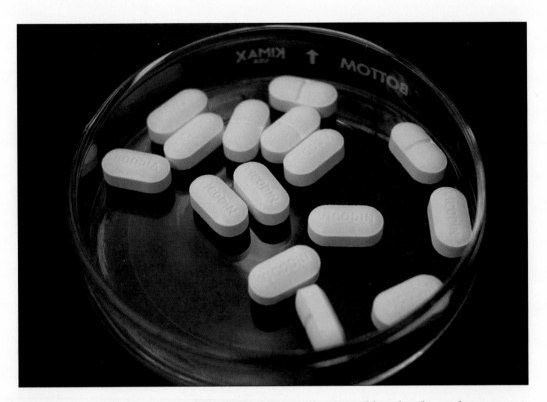

*Hydrocodone is an opioid pain medication. These pills were sold under the trade name Vicodin.*

Short term use produces muddled thinking, dry mouth, heavy feeling in limbs, nausea and vomiting, severe itching, and in some cases respiratory failure due to the slowdown of breathing. Long-term use produces pus-filled infections (abscesses), collapsed veins, heart infections, liver disease, pneumonia and other lung diseases, clogging of blood vessels due to additives, HIV, hepatitis B, and hepatitis C from using contaminated needles, and death from respiratory failure.

As the cycle of addiction goes from regular use of substances, to tolerance of them, to the need to increase amounts and shorten the duration between doses, and finally to dependence, or addiction. Withdrawal occurs when the substance has not been taken in too long a period of time. As mentioned before, it involves a range of symptoms, from cravings for the drug to restlessness, diarrhea, vomiting, sneezing, chills with goose bumps, muscle pain and spasms, kicking movements, depression, anxiety, and insomnia. In *Thinking Simply About Addiction*, author and psychiatrist Richard S. Sandor, M.D. says, "Withdrawals from opiates triggers one of the most powerful hungers known to human beings."

---

 ## Text-Dependent Questions

1. How are synthetic opioids different from natural ones?
2. What factors affect the intensity of an opioid high?
3. What are the steps in the cycle of addiction?

---

 ## Research Project

Since the spike in opioid addictions and fatalities, many local and national governments are urging physicians to restrict the use of these painkillers. However, those who live with chronic pain daily worry about such restrictions. Consult online sources such as the Pain News Network (www.painnewsnetwork.org) to learn about these worries. Then, summarize what you have learned in a short essay.

 **Words to Understand in This Chapter**

domestic violence—abuse or aggressive behavior that occurs inside the home, usually between couples who live together.

sexually transmitted diseases—also called STDs, these are diseases or infections which are transmitted through sexual contact.

substance abuse—dependence on addictive substances like alcohol, opioids, or other drugs.

under the influence—the state of being impaired by alcohol or drug use.

*Drug overdose is the leading cause of accidental death in the United States. Of the approximately 50,000 lethal drug overdoses that occur each year, more than 60 percent are caused by opioid pain relievers or heroin.*

**3**

# When It Becomes a Problem

At first, opioid use may seem to have only positive effects to the user. The rush and euphoria are pleasurable. The ability to "check out" of the realities of life is attractive to many. When people become addicted, though, the negative effects begin to pile up. We've covered health effects in the previous chapter. What about other effects, though?

Relationships become strained. Addiction causes people to do and say things they would normally not do. They may ask friends or family members for money. They may ask people close to them to lie and cover for them. When sources of money dry up they may steal from friends and family, and others in the community. Drugs are expensive and as the addiction intensifies, with the need of higher and more frequent doses, the costs rise. Addicts can lose jobs because of positive drug tests, erratic behavior, or absences from work. They can lose their homes or apartments because they can't keep up with the mortgage or rent. Schoolwork can be too difficult to keep up with, and sporadic attendance makes it harder to absorb the material. Dropping out of school is common. Sometimes, addicts end up trading sex for drugs or becoming prostitutes.

These activities lead to arrests by law enforcement. Jail time, probation requirements, fines, court-ordered rehab, all these are life-changing. Addicts' personal safety is frequently at risk. The drug trade attracts criminals, who may be violent or otherwise abusive. Accidents and injuries can result from behavior addicts perform while *under the influence*. The risk of infectious diseases is high, especially when needles are shared. This makes it easy for serious diseases like HIV to pass between people. *Sexually transmitted diseases* or unwanted pregnancies may also result when addicts find themselves acting out of the ordinary. Depression and other mental disorders can be made worse by addiction, too.

## What Addiction Does to Families

A person's drug use and abuse hurts families in many ways, some of them lasting. It puts a lot of stress on all members of the home, from parents, to siblings, grandparents, and children. Drug abuse means that family members cannot count on addicts to do what they say they will do. Addicts may lie, steal, get fired from their jobs, and disappear for days at a time.

*Opioid abuse takes a devastating toll on families, with addicted parents more prone to violence or more likely to neglect or abuse their young children.*

Families may fight a lot because of these problems, and they may be ashamed by the addict's bad behavior and brushes with the law. They may experience a range of emotions by the addict's actions: anger, fear, concern, embarrassment, and guilt. Families may demand that addicts stop talking to them, or want nothing further to do with them.

The effects of addiction on children can be devastating. When a parent is incapacitated by drug use, children may have to take on the roles that parents should, like preparing meals and other household chores. They may have to worry about

# Growing Up with Drug Addict Parents

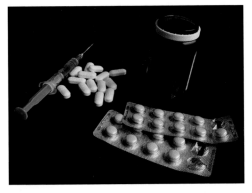

User SomeoneOutThere on ExperienceProject.com provides riveting details about growing up surrounded by addiction. Her parents met at a methadone clinic where they were being treated for opioid addiction. Her mother was a nurse who started using drugs when she stole pills from the hospitals she worked for. Both parents would take her along when they went to buy marijuana. When she was around 10 years old, her father would come home in different moods daily. She remembers her parents arguing in the car. She stuck her head out the window so that she wouldn't hear them.

When she was 11 her father committed suicide. Her mother began using drugs heavily. She would pass out on the floor and would not wake up until cold water was poured on her head. Once her mother fell asleep in a car and the police came. They called child protective services and an investigation was launched.

After a while, her mother no longer tried to hide her drug use. Her mother's drug dealer became her boyfriend, and they would use drugs in front of the kids. Their house caught on fire and they moved to motels. After about a year her mother got arrested. She and her younger brother were sent to foster care. Soon afterward, her mother overdosed and died on the street. All this chaos marred SomeoneOutThere's childhood, but she made the decision to steer clear of all drugs, which gave her a brighter future.

keeping food in the house, utilities like electricity on, and becoming homeless. They may need to deal with the addict's unsavory acquaintances. They may not have rules or boundaries of right and wrong and need to deal with other forms of parental neglect. The overall environment of the home is often negative, filled with complaints, criticism, and bad moods. To put it simply, parents who are addicts put their need to obtain and use drugs before their children's health and welfare. Children may be abused physically or emotionally. They may lack proper immunization, medical care, dental treatment, and the basic necessities of food, water, and shelter.

Children who grow up in such environments experience long term difficulties with relationships and may fall into *substance abuse* themselves or choose substance abusers as mates.

When a pregnant woman abuses drugs, the baby inside of her is also affected. The baby may be born underweight, have difficulty eating and sleeping, have problems with eyesight, hearing, and movement, and might be overall slow to develop. As the child grows, he or she might have difficulty following directions, paying attention, learning in school, and getting along with others. The child may act out violently and need

 **Did You Know?**

NAMI, the National Alliance on Mental Illness, reports that more than half of all drug addicts also experience some form of mental illness.

special teachers and schools. They may need special care throughout their lives.

## What Addiction Does to Society

The costs to society of substance abuse are steep: nearly $200 billion due to costs related to crime, health care, and diminished productivity at work. Crime involves *domestic violence*, theft, assault, and the possession and trafficking of illegal drugs. Crime is not just committed by drug addicts; they are

*According to the US Department of Justice, which oversees the federal prison system, approximately half of all inmates in federal prisons are serving time for drug-related offenses. In state prisons, more than 200,000 inmates are incarcerated on drug charges as of 2017. This is roughly 16 percent of the total population of the state prison systems.*

**Educational Video**

For a short film on abuse of heroin
and prescription pills, scan here:

often victims as well. The latest statistics collected by the
Federal Bureau of Prisons shows that nearly 50 percent of
inmates are in prison due to drug offenses. The cost to taxpay-
ers to fund the prison system, corrections officers, police officers, judicial officials and others is staggering. Law enforcement attacks drugs with a three-pronged effort that involves
targeting smugglers, sellers, and users. A large part of this
involves keeping international shipments of opioids out of the
country by customs officials, border patrol, and others.

Health care for drug addicts is a huge cost, due to the medical problems that come from addiction, and costs for rehabilita-
tion. These involve costs from doctor-shopping--when prescription pain pill addicts try to get prescriptions from numerous

 **Did You Know?**

According to the National Institute on Drug Abuse (NIDA), a baby is
born suffering from opioid withdrawal every 25 minutes.

*The National Institute on Drug Abuse reported in 2017 that abuse of tobacco, alcohol, and illicit drugs exacts more than $700 billion annually in costs related to crime, lost work productivity, and health care.*

doctors to feed their habit--emergency room visits, and treatment for illnesses and injuries. A 2007 study put the cost of prescription painkiller abuse up to $72.5 billion for insurers, who then pass the increased costs along to customers. Many addicts who are homeless and jobless use state and federal welfare and healthcare subsidies, which raise costs to taxpayers, too.

The workplace suffers due to impaired employees, who put extra burdens on coworkers and lower overall productivity.

Some positions, such as airline pilots, train operators, and bus drivers, if they are occupied by impaired individuals, can lead to injuries and fatalities to the public. Other accidents may also occur at work due to drug abuse. The increased use of medical and insurance benefits by employees who abuse drugs also leads to increased costs.

 **Text-Dependent Questions**

1. What are at least seven effects addiction has on addicts?
2. How does an addict's behavior affect their family?

 **Research Project**

NIDA has created an number of infographics related to drug use and abuse. Choose one from this page:

https://www.drugabuse.gov/related-topics/trends-statistics/infographics

and summarize the findings in a one-page essay.

 **Words to Understand in This Chapter**

benzodiazepines—a class of drugs used as tranquilizers; Valium is one such example.

cognitive behavioral therapy—a type of psychotherapy that helps patients challenge and change negative thought patterns.

hypnotics—a sleep-inducing drug such as Ambien or Lunesta.

4

# Preventing Problems

The difficult facts about opioid addiction and the havoc it wreaks on addicts' lives, their families, and society at large can make addiction seem like a death sentence. Indeed, it is a challenging hole to crawl out of, but there are reasons for hope that we will discuss in Chapters 5 and 6. The easiest and most effective means of triumphing over opioid addiction is to prevent it from starting in the first place.

More and more, the medical profession and the media at large, are recognizing the role that doctors and pharmaceutical companies have played in the opioid addiction epidemic. Opioid prescription has become a common practice. The CDC reports that, "In 2012, health care providers wrote 259 million prescriptions for opioid pain medication, enough for every adult in the United States to have a bottle of pills." The CDC estimates that one in five patients who visit doctors' offices reporting pain that is not associated with cancer receive an opioid prescription. Due to this overprescription of opioids, and the fact that such prescribing can vary amongst states, the CDC has issued updated guidelines for the prescribing of opioids for chronic pain. This updated report, published in March 2016, aims to provide physicians with guidelines for assisting patients who experience chronic pain. This includes a checklist and a website focusing on the subject, as well as other tools.

 ## Clean and Sober in Iceland

Twenty years ago, Iceland had a problem. Hard drinking teens were everywhere. "You couldn't walk the streets in downtown Reykjavik on a Friday night because it felt unsafe. There were hordes of teenagers getting in-your-face drunk," says Harvey Milkman, a psychology professor.

Milkman's work on his doctorate had given him some insight into substance abuse. He concluded that people choose to abuse drugs depending on what sort of stress they were dealing with at the time. Those who wanted to become numb used heroin. Those who wanted to confront their stress actively used amphetamines. While he was at Metropolitan State College of Denver, Milkman developed his ideas further. Kids who wanted a rush—the active confronters—would either get it through stimulant drugs or stimulating behavior, like stealing radios or tires or even cars.

Milkman then wondered if a society could produce natural highs for people. That way the people would not suffer the terrible effects of

It is not just physicians that need to be aware of prescription practices, though. Patients themselves should become educated about what drugs they are taking. Other medication and treatment may work better with fewer risks and side effects than opioids. These include acetaminophen, ibuprofen, physical therapy, exercise, medication for depression or seizures, and *cognitive behavioral therapy*.

Patients should also be aware that if prescribed opioids they should follow these guidelines: only use them as prescribed-- never take more doses than your doctor specifies. Drugs such

---

drug addiction. It wasn't enough to just give people information about the dangers of drugs and alcohol because evidence had shown that this was ineffective. An Icelandic colleague of Milkman's, Inga Dóra Sigfúsdóttir, wondered whether a program could be designed to give kids healthy alternatives to drugs and alcohol before they began to take them in the first place?

Iceland officials signed on enthusiastically. The program, called Youth in Iceland, set curfews for 13–16 year olds, changed laws to make buying tobacco illegal for those under 18 years of age and alcohol to those under 20, and encouraged parents to spend more time weekly with their children. They also increased funding for sports, music, art, dance, and other types of clubs. The results were astounding. In 1998, 42 percent of 15 and 16 year olds had been drunk in any given month. In 2016 that number had dropped to just 5 percent. Cannabis use dropped from 17 percent to 7 percent, and smoking cigarettes daily went from 23 percent to 3 percent.

*Studies indicate that young men are more likely to experiment with illegal drugs than are young women.*

as alcohol, *benzodiazepines*, muscle relaxants, *hypnotics*, or other opioid pain relievers should be avoided. Do not share pills with others, and make sure to follow up with your doctor regularly.

A 2015 University of Michigan study reported that, "High school students who legitimately use an opioid prescription are one-third more likely to misuse the drug by age 23 than those with no history of the prescription." The study's results are particularly important to consider due to the fact that the US Food and Drug Administration recently decided to approve use of OxyContin for children ages 11 to 16.

The conclusion is clear: no matter your age group, be careful about what you put in your body, whether it comes from doctors or friends. Ask questions and learn the risks first.

## Education Matters

The University of Michigan runs a multi-year study on many drug-related topics known as the Monitoring the Future study. In 2016, the figures were updated for the study named "Narcotics other than Heroin: Trends in Annual Use and Availability for Grades 8, 10, and 12." The percentage of students who listed narcotics as easy to get is as follows: 19 percent for grade 8, 15 percent for grade 10, and 40 percent for grade 12. More statistics are available for heroin use in the 8th, 10th, and 12th grades. Heroin was listed as easy to get for 15 percent of 8th graders, 17 percent of 9th graders, and 20 percent of 12th graders. Eighth through 12th graders who disapprove of using heroin once or twice ranges between 85 and 95 percent. However, the risk of those same students actually using once or twice is quite high as well, between 60 and 75 percent.

 **Educational Video**

Scan here for an interactive video on drug use decisions:

# Substance Abuse Risk Factors

A risk factor is something that increases your chance of experiencing some event or condition, in this case drug addiction. Just because you have a risk factor that does not mean you will develop an addiction or condition, it just increases the chance that you will. These include:

- A family history of addiction. This could mean that you inherited a tendency to become addicted to drugs or alcohol.
- Gender. Males are more likely to develop drug problems than females. However, when females become addicts their disease progresses more quickly than in males.
- Having a mental health condition. Depression, ADHD, or other conditions make a person more prone to substance abuse.
- Peer pressure. Pressure from friends and other peers to use drugs and alcohols can up your risk of addiction.
- Family problems. If your family is not involved in your life, if they are experiencing conflicts, unemployment, or other stressful events, or if you are not supervised enough your risk for substance abuse increases.
- Poverty. Poverty creates difficulties in life that you may want to escape through substance abuse.

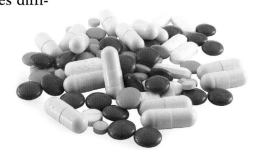

While it is important for students to learn about the harmful effects of opioids, these numbers show that education alone is not enough to keep a large percentage from trying it once or twice. The problem with such usage is that for some people, once or twice is all it takes to get hooked.

## Wide Level Prevention

Now that the scope of opioid addiction has become clear, governmental agencies, medical organizations, and nonprofit institutes have begun working on preventing addiction on a wide level across society. These efforts include educating health care professionals and patients on the dangers of opioid prescriptions, instituting laws to detect when addicts try to doctor-shop or pharmacy-shop, or move from provider to provider in order to obtain increased prescriptions, and encouraging physicians to urge patients into opioid treatment. Other efforts include a requirement to present a photo ID to pick up opioid prescriptions at the pharmacy, drug testing suspected users' urine, providing for safe disposal of opioid prescription medicine that is

---

 **Did You Know?**

The National Institutes of Health agency NIDA has this to say about addiction. "Drug addiction is a preventable disease. Results from NIDA-funded research have shown that prevention programs involving families, schools, communities, and the media are effective in reducing drug abuse."

unused, and increased medical referrals to substance abuse specialists and pain clinics.

Drug manufacturers are also taking steps to prevent people from altering drugs so that they can be snorted or injected. Physical or chemical barriers can prevent pills from being crushed, ground up, or dissolved. Substances can be included with pills that makes them ineffective if they are damaged or that create unpleasant effects if the drug is taken at different levels than prescribed. Long-acting injections allow for slow release of the drug over a long period of time instead of a quick rush.

The development of safer pain medications that are non-addictive is also in process.

## One on One and Personal Prevention

Parents and guardians play a role in preventing addiction. By showing an interest in their children, spending time with them, and encouraging them to talk share honestly about their problems, stressors, and the presence of drugs in their schools and among their peers, parents can become aware of the realities of their children's lives. Parents should also become aware of the signs of drug addiction, which include isolation from the family, a loss of interest in activities the child previously enjoyed, and theft of money around the home. When parents neglect their children there is a higher risk that the child will abuse substances.

Research shows that young people are less likely use drugs if they keep busy with healthy activities. For instance, adolescents who do volunteer work are 50 percent less likely to use drugs. Students who participate in athletics are 40 percent less likely to use drugs. Other after-school programs also have positive results.

When it comes right down to it, though, whether or not a person decides to take drugs is up to them. Take responsibility for your own behavior and your own body: you have to live in it for the rest of your life. You can choose a difficult, possibly deadly experience, or one that is free of the consequences of drug abuse.

 ## Text-Dependent Questions

1. What do the CDC's updated guidelines for the prescribing of opioids for chronic pain contain?
2. Summarize the findings of the 2016 Monitoring the Future study.
3. What actions are drug manufacturers taking to prevent people from abusing opioids?

 ## Research Project

Many means of preventing drug addiction are presented in this chapter. Choose one and do more in-depth research on it by contacting one of the organizations listed at the back of this book. Aim for learning five facts about the subject that are not covered here. Give an oral report on your findings.

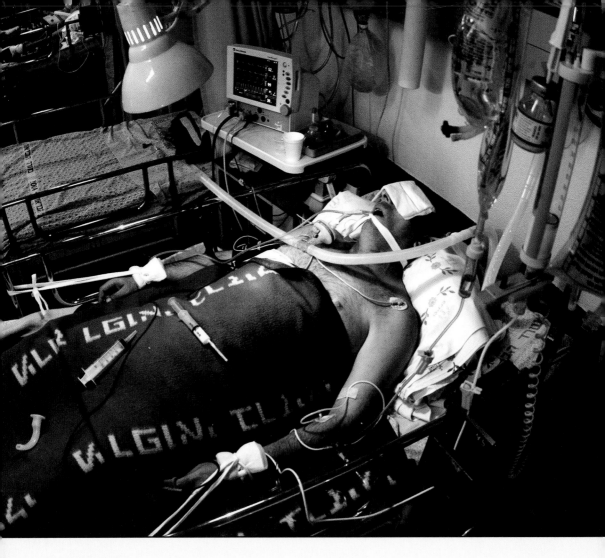

 **Words to Understand in This Chapter**

abstinence—avoidance of the use of drugs or alcohol.

counseling—psychotherapy that occurs between a professional and a patient.

detoxify—to shed a toxin from the body.

relapse—to begin using drugs or alcohol again after a period of non-use.

## 5

In the most severe cases of drug addiction, patients might need to rid their bodies of the drug in a hospital setting. Rapid opioid detoxification treatment is considered to be an effective method of getting people off drugs in the short term.

# In Treatment

Those who fall into opioid addiction have options for treatment. The road toward health and well-being is likely to be rocky, but there are many people and organizations willing to help abusers find their way. What works for one person may not work for another, and *relapse* is a common problem. People who participate in programs may do so inpatient, or as a person who lives in the facility 24 hours a day, or outpatient, as a person who lives elsewhere and comes to a location for meetings. Despite the challenges, many people navigate through the complex system of treatment and exit able to live happy, productive, drug-free lives.

## The First Step

When addicts stop taking their drug of choice they go into withdrawals. They are *detoxifying* their body of the drug. The unpleasant symptoms of withdrawals can be eased by certain medications, and a 2014 study by SAMHSA states that such medications are used in 80 percent of detoxes. Buprenorphine, under the brand name Subutex, or Buprenorphine with naloxone, under the brand name Suboxone, both reduce cravings and other withdrawal symptoms. Often, Subutex is used for initial detox while Suboxone may be used on a maintenance dose to prevent relapse. The blood pressure medicine clonidine does not reduce cravings, but it does calm the brain's "fight or flight" response, which becomes more intense during detox.

Another popular drug for detoxing is methadone, an opioid itself. However, unlike other opioids, it does not provide the opioid rush. It can be used to calm withdrawal effects. On its own, because it is an opioid, it relieves pain. However, because it is an opioid it is also addictive. Many people use methadone during initial detox and then taper off the dose until they are free of it. Others remain on methadone. While they are still addicted to an opioid, they are able to achieve some stability in

 **Educational Video**

To see an addict torn between drugs and his family, scan here:

*Group therapy sessions, in which addicts share their experiences, are often a component of drug treatment programs.*

life because they must visit a medical clinic for their dose on a daily basis. It is less expensive than other opioids, and the stability of a regular routine helps people maintain employment and keep family relationships more harmonious. While it is usually better for addicts to be on methadone maintenance treatment than shooting heroin or using other opioids from the street, it is still a serious drug dependence and should not be approached lightly.

Detox can be achieved by going "cold turkey," or taking no medications and enduring the unpleasant withdrawal effects.

Addicts may choose to undergo this method of detox, or they may have that choice taken away from them if they end up in jail.

## The Next Step

Emerging from drug addiction to *abstinence* is not as simple as detoxing alone for the vast majority of people, who are in danger of relapsing without serious intervention. That intervention comes in the form of behavioral therapies. These therapies help people change their attitudes and behaviors related to opioid abuse, help them increase their skills to combat difficult circumstances and interactions that may trigger a craving for drugs, and provide rewards for remaining abstinent. They come in several varieties, but they usually involve different forms of *counseling*.

## Rewards

Motivational incentives are used for the abuse of opioids, alcohol, and other drugs. They provide patients with rewards for not using drugs. One of these rewards are vouchers. A person receives a voucher every time their urine is drug-tested and it comes up free of drugs, or clean. This voucher is valuable because it can be used for food, movie tickets, and other items. The value of the vouchers increase with every clean drug test the person has. Prize incentives are similar to vouchers, but they involve cash rewards instead. After participants have been in treatment for a period of time—usually at least three months—they can draw a prize from a bowl. These prizes have different values from between $1 and $100. They can also receive other rewards for clean drug tests and attendance at counseling sessions.

## CRA Plus Vouchers

Community Reinforcement Approach (CRA) Plus Vouchers refers to an intense 24-week outpatient program. The goal is to help attendants practice abstinence in order to learn life skills that will help protect them from relapse. Each patient attends up to two individual sessions with a therapist. During these sessions they cover improving relationships within the family, learning job skills, helping them to acquire new friend net-

 **Barriers to Treatment**

Each year, a small percentage of opioid addicts receive the treatment that they desperately need. Why is this? Due to barriers to treatment, or obstacles that keep people from getting help. The biggest of these obstacles, at about 95 percent, is that the users do not believe that they need treatment. Instead, they allow their addiction to control their lives. Many users realize that they need treatment, but they were not able to receive it either because they lacked health insurance or because they could not afford the cost of treatment. In 2013, 316,000 addicted persons tried to get treatment, but more than 37 percent of them were prevented from getting it due to cost. Even those who did have health insurance were not guaranteed that addiction treatment would be covered. Many people also worry about what effect long-term treatment will have on their schoolwork, jobs, or families, so they avoid treatment.

## Did You Know?

In 1997, the National Institutes of Health (NIH) published a report on effective medical treatment of opiate addiction. Regarding the use of methadone, it said, "Prolonged oral treatment with this medication diminishes and often eliminates opiate use, reduces transmission of many infections, including HIV and hepatitis B and C, and reduces criminal activity."

works, and develop new forms of recreation to replace drug use. Vouchers are given out for clean urine samples, which are tested several times a week. These vouchers allow participants to "buy" store goods that help them maintain a drug-free life. A similar program exists online called the Therapeutic Education System (TES).

## Narcotics Anonymous

Narcotics Anonymous, or NA, is a self-help program known as a twelve-step program. The original twelve-step program was Alcoholics Anonymous, or AA. AA was formed in 1935. The basis of the program is a series of twelve steps that are a group of spiritual principles which are designed to become a way of life without dependence on alcohol. AA has meetings worldwide and is for anyone who has a drinking problem. They are anonymous in that members identify themselves by their first names, and what happens in meetings is kept confidential. NA is modeled after AA, except that it is not limited to alcohol but instead embraces abusers of any "mood-changing, mind-altering substance." NA is quick to state that they are not affiliated with any particular religion, instead adhering to spiritual principles. Finally, people may either not know where to receive treatment or not be able to enter a treatment program due to long waiting lists.

In twelve-step programs like NA participants will be introduced to three key ideas. The first is acceptance that participants have a chronic, progressive disease that they have no control over, and as a result their lives have become unmanageable. Willpower is not enough to overcome the problem. Abstinence is the only remedy to this disease. The second idea is that the participant must give themselves over to a higher power of their choice, accept the support and fellowship of other group members, and follow the steps laid out in the program. Finally, members must become actively involved in their own recovery, participating in meetings and helping others when possible.

As of 2014, NA held more than 63,000 weekly meetings in 132 countries. The 2013 NA membership survey reported that the average length of abstinence for members was 11.07 years. Before coming to NA, 42 percent of members reported that

 **Did You Know?**

SAMHSA reports that in 2015, 21.7 million people were in need of substance abuse treatment during the prior year. However, only about 11 percent of them, or 2.3 million people, received such treatment.

they were incapable of holding down a job, having their own place of residence, maintaining family relationships, supporting their children, and preserving committed, intimate relationships. Once members committed to regular attendance at meetings and full participation in the program 92 percent reported improvement in family relationships, 76 percent reported improvement in stable housing, and 72 percent reported improvement in their employment situation. It is clear from NA's popularity that, like they say in the program, it works if you work it.

## Family Therapy

Another dimension to drug treatment is Family Behavioral Therapy, or FBT. The idea behind this form of counseling is that substance abuse problems occur alongside other problems in the family. These problems can be mental health disorders, child abuse, violence, and job loss. Therapists work to help affected families to improve the functioning of their lives. This can involve many types of work, such as having parents who abuse substances themselves set goals to parent more effectively. Patients work with therapists to set goals to improve their lives, with the idea that accomplishing such goals will result in less temptation to abuse drugs.

## Adolescent Therapy

In addition to family therapy, young people often have different needs that are addressed in therapy programs designed specifically for adolescents. A number of issues are covered that influence the patient's substance abusing behavior. These include the patient's, and possibly their peers', favorable attitude toward drugs, conflict in the family, poor discipline practices, substance abuse by other family members, poor performance in school, and dangerous conditions in their neighborhoods. Such therapy has reduced participants' drug use during and after treatment, and lowered their rate of incarceration.

Another approach in adolescent therapy involves the therapist working with patients to help them make good decisions, solve problems, and learn how to negotiate. Patients learn job skills and how to communicate to lower stress. Parents also learn how to support their child during this therapy.

 **Text-Dependent Questions**

1. What is the first step in a drug abuse treatment program?
2. What are the pros and cons of using methadone for opioid addiction?
3. Why is family therapy an important part of a drug abuse treatment program?

 **Research Project**

Use the internet, newspapers, or magazines in order to research the drug naloxone (brand name Narcan) and the effect it has on opioid overdose victims. Design and create a pamphlet that illustrates the information you have found.

Drug Enforcement Administration
**Good Medicine, Bad Behavior:**
Drug Diversion in America

Joseph Rannazzisi

Sharon A. Brigner

 **Words to Understand in This Chapter**

chronic—a problem that lasts a long time.

enable—to solve problems for addicts so that they do not face the consequences of their behavior.

intervention—an effort by an addict's friends and family to confront them about their addiction so that they choose to get help.

6

# Helping an Addict

The preceding chapters provide a lot of information about the difficulties of the opioid abuse epidemic. There are things that everyday people can do about the epidemic, though. First, educate yourself about the disease. Learn how to identify whether someone you care about has a problem. Observe whether someone is getting rid of withdrawal symptoms by using drugs again, becoming tolerant to the substance, continuing to use drugs even when aware of the damage they are causing, neglecting responsibilities to family and home, and appearing sick. Other danger signs are spending a lot of time obtaining, using, and recovering from the drug, trying to cut down the dosage but being unable to do so, and continuing to use drugs even if they make a physical or mental problem worse. It can take careful observation over a period of days or weeks to learn whether a person is experiencing these problems.

Speak with friends or family members to see what they think about the person's behavior. If they agree that there is a problem, decide together who will talk to the person about getting help. Do not try to speak to someone about a drug problem when they are under the influence of drugs or alcohol. Make sure that you approach the situation carefully. Confronting the person may cause an argument because people often deny that they have a problem. If that is the case you can contact the person's doctor and ask if they would be willing to speak with him or her about addiction. In the United States today there are 3,500 board-certified physicians who specialize in addiction.

It takes a lot of courage for a person to seek help for a drug problem. People often worry about what others will think or about what will happen to them physically once they are no longer taking drugs. Or they may have tried treatment before and relapsed. People who are unwilling to enter treatment are often pressured to do so by their family or friends, or made to do so by the justice system. Staging an intervention to convince someone they have a problem can turn into a fight and end up doing more harm than good. Develop a safety plan for yourself in case of threats or violence.

When you approach someone about a drug problem it is important to try to have a back and forth conversation with the person, not a lecture. Try to keep from judging the person but do express that you are worried about them.

# Narateen

In 1951, Lois W., the wife of Bill W., co-founder of Alcoholics Anonymous, founded a group called Al-Anon. Its purpose is to help the friends and family of alcoholics deal with, triumph over, and share stories with those who care about addicts. By modifying the twelve steps and twelve traditions of Alcoholics Anonymous, Al-Anon quickly grew popular. Over time, a subgroup called Alateen was established. As a part of Al-Anon, it focuses on the special needs of teenaged friends and family members of alcoholics.

After Narcotics Anonymous was founded to help narcotics addicts, Nar-anon also came into existence to help their friends and families. Just like with Alateen, a teen version of Narcotics Anonymous was founded, called Narateen. Narateen is a support group that helps teens gain peace of mind, coping skills, and hope to deal with a loved one's addiction. Everyone who attends uses only their first names in order to keep their identities anonymous. No one is forced to speak in the meetings, but listening to the stories of other members helps participants be part of a group that understands them like no one else can.

An anonymous Narateen member has this to say about the pro-gram: "I can be happy ... I was so sad about my dad using drugs. I was afraid when my mom and dad would argue. Since I came to Narateen, I was happy to learn that it's not my fault. It's okay for me to be happy even if mom and dad are not."

Unfortunately, there is no quick and easy fix for drug addiction, so it is wise to prepare yourself for the fact that the process can be lengthy.

## What About You?

When you care about someone with an addiction, life can be painful. It is easy to believe that you should do something to help that person, like give them money, a place to live, or cover for them in school or even on the job. But the line between helping and hurting can be thin, especially when it comes to addictions. Often friends and loved ones actually enable that person to avoid the consequences of their addiction by thinking that they are helping them.

It can seem strange to look for help for yourself when there is an addict in your life, but it can be hard to deal with an addict's erratic behavior. Friends and family of addicts may blame themselves and take the burden of someone's addictions on their own shoulders. The difficulty can be demonstrated by this quote from Nar-Anon program literature:

We become detectives and search the premises and their personal belongings for drugs and drug-related items. We

 ## Educational Video

To understand why it is so hard to quit drugs, scan here:

*According to a 2014 Pew Research Center study, 26 percent of Americans want the government to focus more on prosecuting illegal drug users, while 67 percent of them want the government to focus more on providing treatment for illegal drug users.*

become obsessed with where they are, what they are doing, and how we might control their addiction. We want to believe the problem can solve itself even though our gut feeling tells us this is not so. We want to believe the addicts' promises, but common sense tells us there is something wrong. We become victims of denial.

## Did You Know?

Relapse rates for drug addicts is 40 to 60 percent, according to the *Journal of American Medicine*, a similar rate to other chronic diseases such as Type I Diabetes (30 to 50 percent), hypertension (50 to 70 percent), and asthma (50 to 70 percent.)

By learning effective strategies to deal with addicts, and by caring for your own needs, you will be able to achieve a calmness and strength that will end up not only benefitting you but also your interactions with the addicted person you care for. One of the ways you can learn such strategies, and obtain support from people who understand what you are going through, is by attending a Nar-Anon group meeting in your area. Nar-Anon is a twelve-step program for the friends and family of a narcotics addict. Like the Narcotics Anonymous program, which is for the addict themselves, Nar-Anon provides a spiritual, but non-religious, self-help group that seeks to help lighten the load that chronic addiction places on the friends and family of addicts by sharing members' "experience, strength, and hope."

Since one size fits all does not apply when it comes to substance abuse, other, non-spiritual programs and self-help groups are also available, though they are smaller than Nar-Anon. Examples are SMART Recovery and Rational Recovery.

Another way to care for yourself is to express your feelings through creative activities. Writing, painting, sculpture, playing a musical instrument, dancing, woodworking, and other creative pursuits can help you to make something new and unique and enjoy yourself at the same time. One high-profile example of such creativity is the GRAMMY Foundation and MusiCares annual Teens Make Music Contest for the composition of an original song or music video that brings attention to the consequences of substance abuse or celebrates a drug-free life.

 **Text-Dependent Questions**

1. How can you know if your friend or loved one has a drug problem?
2. What effect does enabling an addict's bad behavior have on them?
3. Why can it be helpful to take up a creative activity?

 **Research Project**

Research the annual Teens Make Music contest sponsored by the GRAMMY Foundation and MusiCares at http://abovetheinfluence.com/grammys/. Watch videos of the previous winners at this site and listen to the lyrics and songs of some previous winners at the Partnership for a Drug Free America at http://drugfree.org/newsroom/news-item/teen-musicians-win-grammy-foundation-musicares-teens-make-music-contest-59th-annual-grammy-awards-experience/. Next, come up with your own song, poem, drawing, painting, or other creative project that relates to the effects of substance abuse.

# Series Glossary

**analgesic**—any member of a class of drugs used to achieve analgesia, or relief from pain.

**central nervous system**—the part of the human nervous system that consists of the brain and spinal cord. These are greatly affected by opiates and opioids.

**dependence**—a situation that occurs when opiates or opioids are used so much that the user's body adapts to the drug and only functions normally when the drug is present. When the user attempts to stop using the drug, a physiologic reaction known as withdrawal syndrome occurs.

**epidemic**—a widespread occurrence of a disease or illness in a community at a particular time.

**opiates**—a drug that is derived directly from the poppy plant, such as opium, heroin, morphine, and codine

**opioids**—synthetic drugs that affect the body in a similar way as opiate drugs. The opioids include Oxycotin, hydrocodone, fentanyl, and methadone.

**withdrawal**—a syndrome of often painful physical and psychological symptoms that occurs when someone stops using an addictive drug, such as an opiate or opioid. Often, the drug user will begin taking the drug again to avoid withdrawal.

# Further Reading

Gammill, Joani. *Painkillers, Heroin, and the Road to Sanity*. Center City, MN: Hazelden, 2014.

Parks, Peggy J. *Heroin Addiction*. San Diego, CA: Referencepoint Press, 2015.

Portwood, Amber. *Never Too Late*. New York, NY: Post Hill Press, 2014.

Quinones, Sam. *Dreamland: The True Tale of America's Opiate Epidemic*. New York: Bloomsbury, 2015.

Reed, Amy. *Clean*. New York, NY: Simon Pulse, 2012.

Rodriguez, Ray. *Overcoming Prescription Drug Addiction*. Palm Springs, FL: Stepping Up Recovery, LLC, 2015.

Roos, Stephen. *A Young Person's Guide To The Twelve Steps*. Hazelden Publishing, 1992.

Stolberg, Victor B. *Painkillers: History, Science, and Issues*. California: ABC-CLIO, 2016.

Taylor, Donald R. *Managing Patients with Chronic Pain and Opioid Addiction*. New York: Springer, 2015.

# Internet Resources

**https://teens.drugabuse.gov**

National Institute on Drug Abuse for Teens features drug facts, videos, games, blog posts, and more about staying clean.

**http://www.drugfree.org/stories-of-hope**

Stories of Hope features personal stories of those who have been touched by addiction.

**https://www.justthinktwice.gov**

Just Think Twice is created by the DEA and features personal stories of young addicts, facts about drug use, research highlights about drugs, videos, and quizzes.

**https://www.dosomething.org/us**

Billed as a global movement for good, this site provides links to volunteer opportunities for teens.

---

*Publisher's Note: The websites listed on these pages were active at the time of publication. The publisher is not responsible for websites that have changed their address or discontinued operation since the date of publication. The publisher reviews and updates the websites each time the book is reprinted.*

**http://www.nar-anon.org/narateen**

Narateen is a self-help group for teens whose friends or family are addicted to narcotics. It follows the principles of its parent organization Nar-anon.

**http://www.cdc.gov/az/p.html**

The Centers for Disease Control and Prevention website contains an A-Z index that offers comprehensive information on health topics, including painkiller overdose.

**http://www.ccsa.ca/**

This website delivers a wide range of publications on substance abuse in Canada. Subjects relate to prescription drugs, alcohol, youths, treatment, impaired driving, prevention, and standards—among others.

**http://www.samhsa.gov/**

A vast amount of research related to opioids and other substances can be performed on the Substance Abuse and Mental Health Services Administration website. The website also provides resources on national strategies and initiatives, state and local initiatives, and training and education.

**https://www.cihi.ca/en**

The Canadian Institute for Health Information website offers a National Prescription Drug Utilization Information System (NPDUIS) Database that stores pan-Canadian information on public drug programs.

# Index

abstinence, 40, 44, 45, 47
abuse, domestic, 20, 25, 26, 48
addiction, drug
    and abstinence, 40, 44, 45, 47
    costs of, to society, 26–29
    and crimes, 11, 21, 22, 26–27
    and effects on children, 23–26
    and enabling behaviors, 50,
      54–55
    and family relationships, 8, 21,
      22–25, 36, 38–39, 48
    and gender, *34*, 36
    and health risks, 16, 18–19, 22,
      25–26, 27–28, 46
    and mental health, 25, 36, 48
    number of people with, 8, *13*, 47
    and overdoses, 7, 9, 15, *21*
    and peer pressure, 36
    and poverty, *31*, 36
    and pregnancy, 25–26, 27
    and prescription medications,
      10–11, *13, 17*, 27–28, 31–34,
      37–38
    prevention of, 31–35, 37–39
    recognizing signs of, 51–52,
      55–56
    risk factors for, 36, 48–49
    and stress, 8, 32
    and teenagers, 11, *13*, 32–33,
      34–35, 38–39, 48–49
    and tolerance, 10, 18–19
    and unemployment, *7*, 22, 28, *31*
    and withdrawal symptoms, 10,
      19, 42, 43

    *See also* treatment, addiction

behavioral therapies, 30, 33, 44,
    45–46, 48–49
    *See also* treatment, addiction
benzodiazepines, 30, 34
buprenorphine (Subutex), 42

clonidine, 42
codeine, 13, *14*
cognitive behavioral therapy, 30, 33
counseling, 40, 44, 48, 49
    *See also* behavioral therapies
CRA Plus vouchers, 45–46

detoxification, 40, *41*, 42, 43–44
    *See also* treatment, addiction
doctor-shopping, 11, 27–28, 37
doctors
    drug addictions of, 8
    and prescription guidelines,
      31–34, 37, *51*
domestic violence, 20, 25, 26, 48

enabling behaviors, 50, 54–55
endorphins, 14

Family Behavioral Therapy (FBT), 48
family relationships, 8, 21, 22–25, 36,
    38–39
    and therapy, 48, 49
fentanyl, 13, 15

Harrison Narcotics Act, 16

Numbers in **bold italic** refer to captions.

# About the Author

**Xina M. Uhl** is an educational writer who has authored more than twenty nonfiction books. Before becoming a full-time writer, she worked in substance abuse recovery treatment programs for Maricopa County Government in Phoenix, Arizona. She makes her home in southern California, where she enjoys hiking with her three dogs.

**Picture Credits:** DEA photo: 18, 50, 55; United Nations photo: 14; used under license from Shutterstock, Inc.: 1, 6, 13, 17, 23, 24, 26, 28, 34, 36, 43, 53; BravoKilo Video / Shutterstock.com: 30; ChameleonsEye / Shutterstock.com: 38; Leonard Zhukovsky / Shutterstock.com: 20.